The Street Art & Graffiti

Maths book

MATT HORRORS

Copyright © 2018 Matt Horrors

All rights reserved.

ISBN-13: **978-1725065895**

Important notice

If you are one of the artists who feature in this book, please don't have beef with me for unauthorized use of your work. To get permission from each of you would have been a long and arduous task. Instead I prefer to ask for forgiveness. The reason I chose you for this book is a simple one. You have made a difference. Most of you have made a decent living from your talent, some have not. But you all share one thing. The ability to provoke thought through your art.

Please find below website details for all the artists featured in this book. Please take a moment to find out more about them and help spread their work through social media. Most of them deserve more credit than they get.

This is a primarily a Maths book for younger children, however it also provides an opportunity to introduce a new generation to some of lifes hidden geniuses.

I call that a win win..

INVADER: www.space-invaders.com
SUCKLORD: www.suckadelic.com
BANKSY: banksy.co.uk
BORTUSK LEER: www.bortusk.com
ROBOTS WILL KILL: www.robotswillkill.com
BINTY BINT: bintybint.com
CHEO: www.cheo.co.uk
ONECONTINUOUSLINE: ??
SWEET TOOF: sweettoof.com
KAWS: www.kawsone.com
STIK: stik.org
PURE EVIL: www.pureevilclothing.com
D*FACE: www.dface.co.uk
SHEPARD FAIREY: obeygiant.com
BOTJOY: www.botjoy.com
SSOSVA: www.ssosva.com
CRANIO: cranioartes.com
AME72: www.ame72.com
KASHINK: kashink.com
BLEK LE RAT: blekleratoriginal.com
BUFFMONSTER: buffmonster.com
KEITH HARING: www.haring.com

APPARENTLY MASON STORM DOESN'T CONSIDER THE INTERNET DESERVING ENOUGH TO HOST HIS WEBSITE. YOU CAN FIND HIM ON SOCIAL MEDIA IF YOU LOOK HARD ENOUGH.

COUNTING ONE TO TEN

Count how many Invaders there are in each line.

COUNTING ELEVEN TO TWENTY
Count how many Spraycans there are in each line.

SUCKADELIC
THE SUPER SUCKSTORE

Count the toy action figures on each shelf and write the numbers in each box.

GRAFFMATICS

Busy Banksy

Look carefully at this calendar month and write in the missing dates. Count the spray cans to see how many acts of vandalism Banksy has planned.
Then, count how many days he has free.

Sunday	Monday	Tuesday	Wednesday	Thursday	Friday	Saturday
1 massive attack	2 spray can	3	4	5 meeting	6	7 tequila
8	9	10	11 Quiz Night	12	13 massive attack	14 spray can
15 spray can	16	17 meeting	18 massive attack	19 spray can	20	21 tequila
22 massive attack	23 spray can	24	25	26 meeting	27	28 gardening
29	30	31 cards	Acts of vandalism = ☐ Free days = ☐			

7

Monsters and Robots

Count how many Bortusk Leer monsters there are.
Count how many Robots Will Kill there are.

 Monsters   Robots

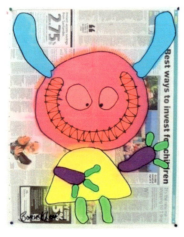

How many Monsters & Robots are there altogether?

The Birds and the Bees

Complete the Binty Bint & Cheo picture sums below. Write the numbers in the boxes.

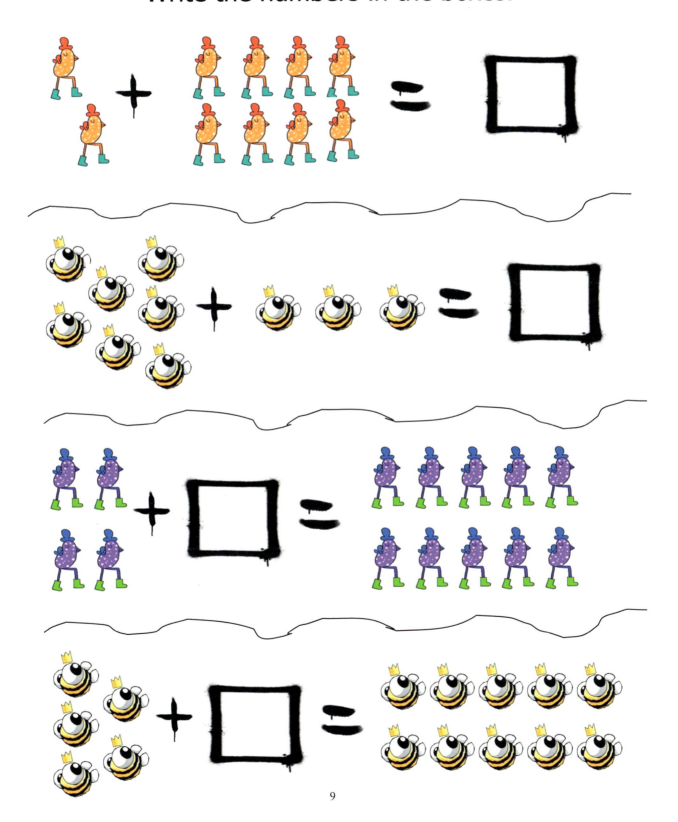

MATT HORRORS

TEN DRUNK OCTOPUS
All want to fight you

Complete the picture sums below.
Write the numbers in the boxes

10

Sweet Toof dental practice

Read the questions and write the answers in the boxes

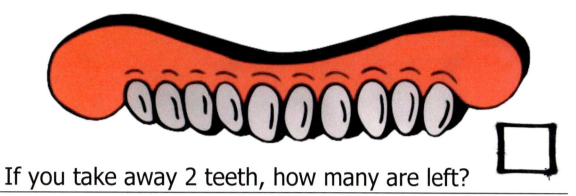

If you take away 2 teeth, how many are left? ☐

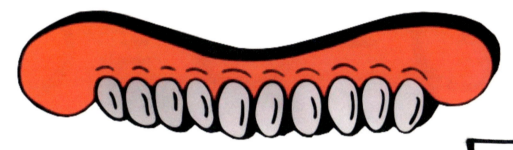

If you take away 4 teeth, how many are left? ☐

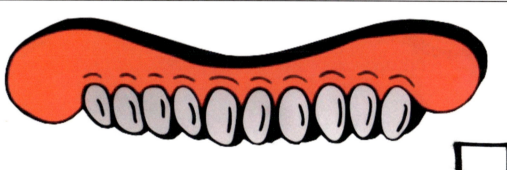

If you take away 5 teeth, how many are left? ☐

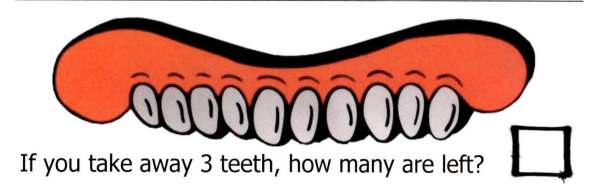

If you take away 3 teeth, how many are left? ☐

Kaws and Effect

Complete the addition and subtraction sums.

17 + 4 =

9 − 6 =

11 + 9 =

13 + 5 =

Balloon Girl

Count the balloons. Draw more so there are 20 in total.

Train Mania

Draw a circle around the highest number on each train carriage.

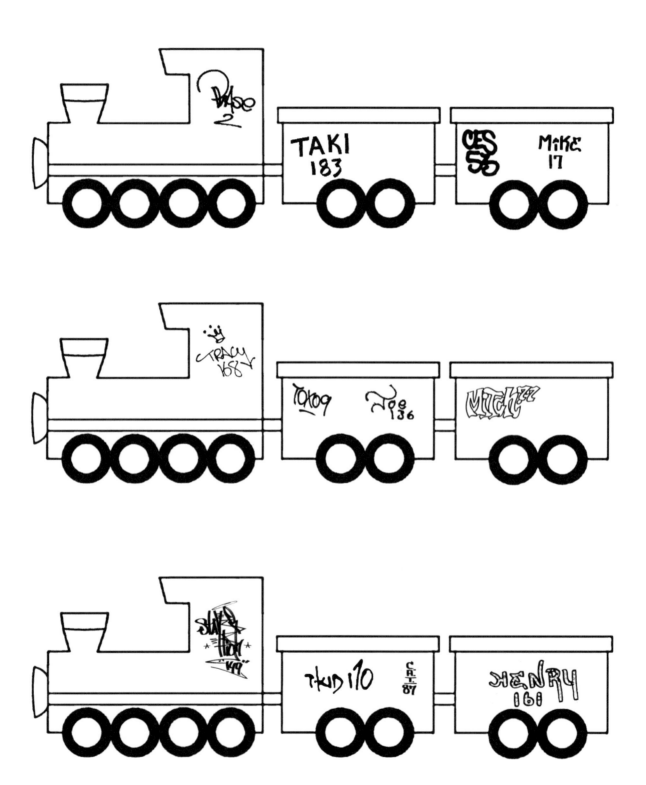

Stik or Twist

Draw a circle around the lowest number in each dancing Stik.

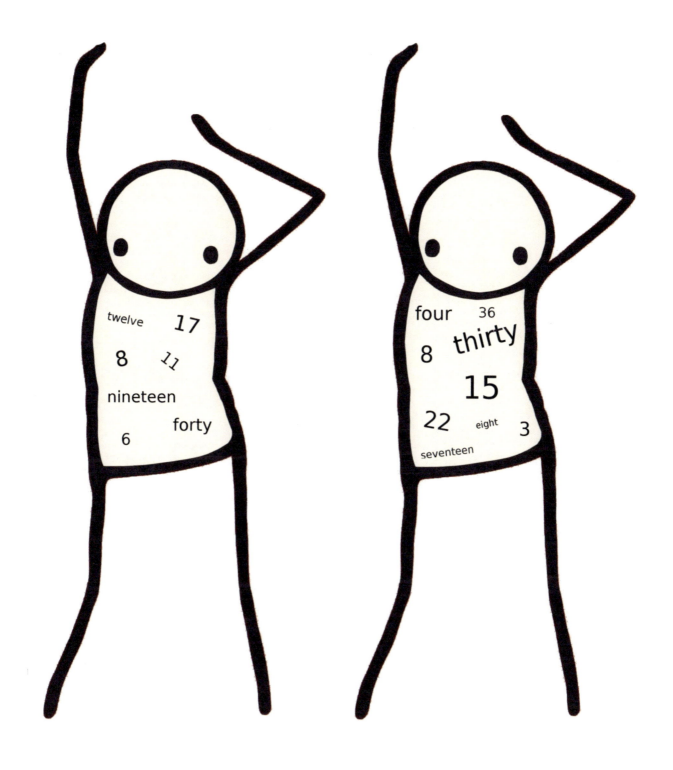

MATT HORRORS

Mason Knows

Mason Storm knows which of these pairs are more or less than each other. He's left an example below.
Look at the rest of the pairs of numbers and write **more** or **less** in the spaces.

Example

17 Bugatti Veyrons are _____Less_____ than **24** Bugatti Veyrons

24 Hublot watches are _____ than **29** Hublot Watches

11 Prada Man bags are _____ than **10** Prada Man bags

19 Gold Skull Rings are _____ than **22** Gold Skull Rings

5 Versace Balaclavas are _____ than **4** Versace Balaclavas

A **63** foot Yacht is _____ than a **56** foot Yacht

Sponsored by

VERSACE

Pure Evil Sums

Do the addition sums and draw lines to the correct answers

Take away with D*Face

Do the subtraction sums and draw lines to the correct answers.

16-12 =

12-6 =

19-14 =

14-11 =

Obey Number Line

Look at the numbers on the Obey stickers. Draw a line from each sticker to the correct place on the number line. Look at the example.

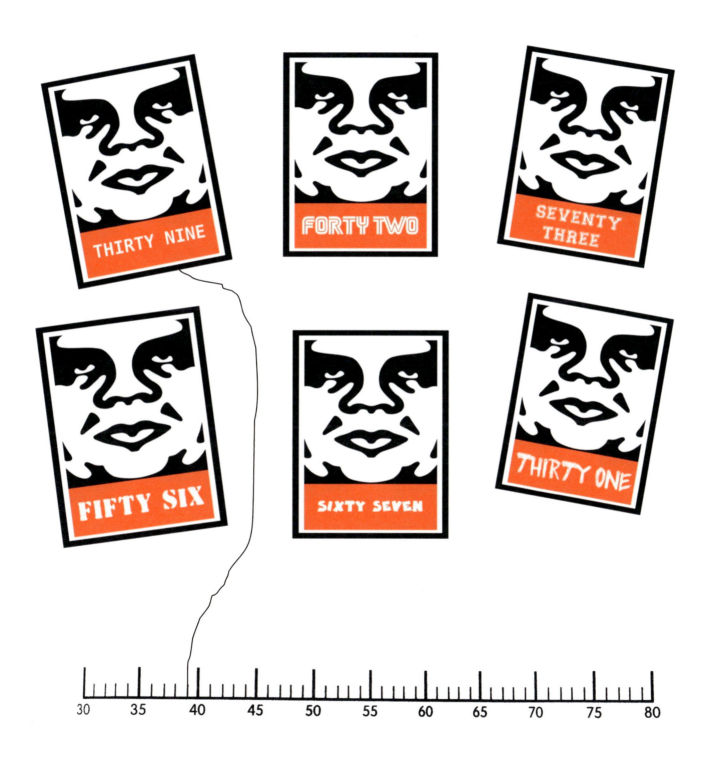

Botjoy Dominoes

Look carefully at the domino pieces **a** to **f**. Use them to play a mini game of dominoes. The aim is to use all 6 pieces. Each pieces has to be next to another domino with the same value (number of dots).
To get started, the first domino has been chosen.

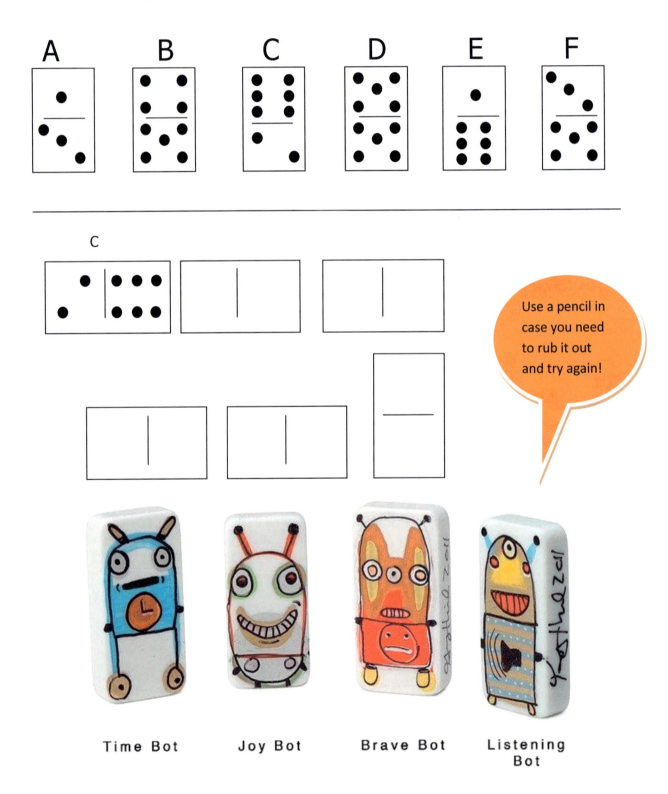

Use a pencil in case you need to rub it out and try again!

Time Bot   Joy Bot   Brave Bot   Listening Bot

SSOSVA

STRENGTH IN NUMBERS

Some numbers are missing in this 100 square.
Fill in the missing numbers.

1	2	3	4	5	6	7	8	9	10
11	12	13		15	16		18	19	20
21		23	24	25		27	28	29	30
	32		34	35	36	37	38	39	40
41	42	43	44	45	46		48		50
	52	53	54		56	57	58	59	60
61	62	63	64		66	67	68		70
71		73	74	75	76	77		79	80
81	82	83		85		87	88	89	90
91	92		94	95	96	97		99	100

The Secret Society of Super Villain Artists.

MATT HORRORS

THE CRANIO
CRANIUM CHALLENGE

Look carefully at the rows of numbers.
Can you see a pattern in each row?
Fill in the missing numbers.

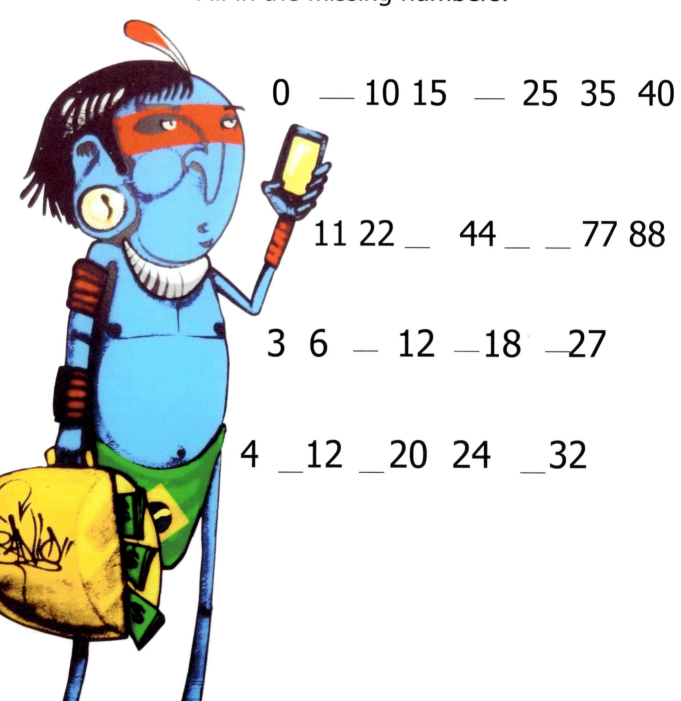

0 __ 10 15 __ 25 35 40

11 22 __ 44 __ __ 77 88

3 6 __ 12 __18 __27

4 __12 __20 24 __32

GRAFFMATICS

AME TO WIN

Write in the missing numbers from AME72 to complete the sum puzzles.

	+	11	=	16
+		+		+
6	+		=	9
=		=		=
11	+	14	=	

12	+	4	=	
-		+		-
10	-		=	8
=		=		=
2	+	6	=	

Think with Kashink

Do the sums and write the answers as words in the crossword grid.

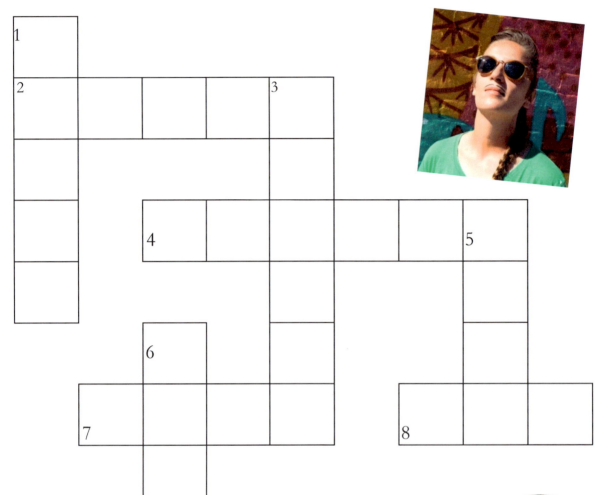

1. 10 − 3 =
2. 4 + 4 =
3. 13 − 1 =
4. 9 + 2 =
5. 15 − 6 =
6. 2 + 4 =
7. 7 − 2 =
8. 14 − 4 =

RATS AnD CATS

There needs to be 10 Blek rats and 10 Superfiend cats.
Draw extra rats and cats so there are 12 of each.

Melty Madness

Complete these Buffmonster Melty addition sums.
Write your answers in the boxes.

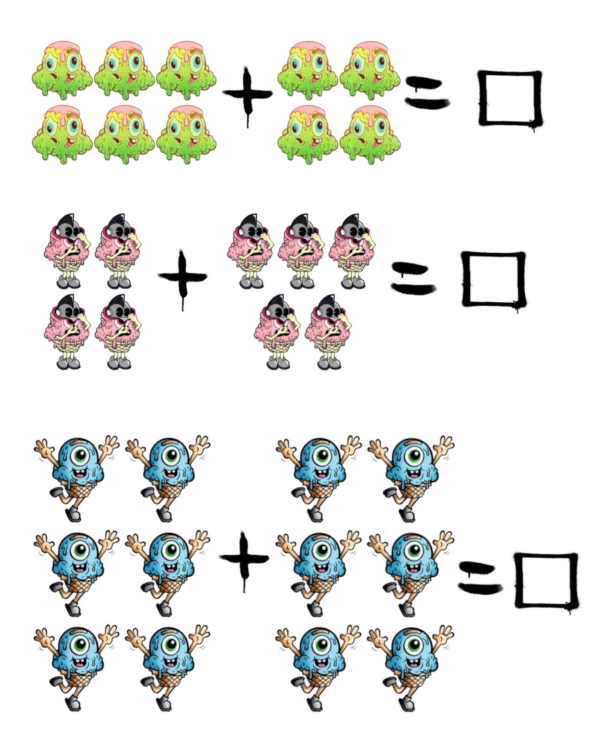

Complicated Keith

Complete these Keith Haring subtraction sums.
Write your answers in the boxes.

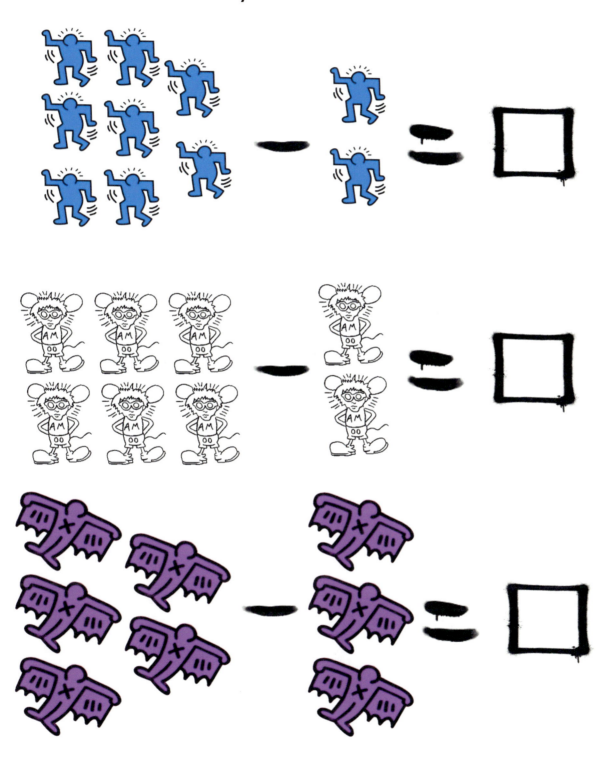

Problems page

Read these problems.
Write your answers in the boxes.

1. On Saturday David Walliams reads 8 pages of the awesome Matt Horrors book "The Battle of East Weezy". On Sunday he read 6 pages. How many pages in total did he read?

2. The Sincura Group stole 3 Banksys in April, 5 Banksys in June and 9 Banksys in September. How many Banksys in total did the Sincura Group steal?

3. Donald Trump made 19 statements of fact at a recent press conference. 4 were true. How many were lies?

4. Andy Council painted a dinosaur made from 25 buildings. The following day 7 of the buildings had been gone over by an idiot toy. How many buildings were left untouched?

Problems page

Read these problems.
Write your answers in the boxes.

5. Mr Brainwash sold 29 pieces of artwork on the first night of his latest show. 2 pieces were made by him. How many were made by other people?

6. On Friday My Dog Sighs left 3 pieces of Free Art Friday on the streets. The following Friday he left 6. The Friday after that he left 8. How many pieces of Free Art Friday did My Dog Sighs leave altogether?

7. Brainfart slapped 9 stickers onto various lamp posts in the middle of the night on Wednesday. Then 12 more on Thursday. How many slaps did they stick to lamp posts in total?

Congrats..
you are now on your way to becoming a Graffmatics superstar.
Like Carol Vorderman

ANSWERS

SUCKADELIC= 1,3,6,8
BUSY BANKSY= 5 acts of vandalism, 14 free days.
MONSTERS & ROBOTS= 6 Monsters, 2 Robots, 8 altogether.
BIRDS & BEES= 10 Chickens, 10 Bees, 14 Chickens, 15 Bees.
DRUNK OCTOPUS= 8, 13, 4, 6
SWEET TOOF DENTIST = 8, 4, 3, 5
KAWS & EFFECT = 21,3, 20, 18
BALLOON GIRL= Draw 2 balloons
TRAIN MANIA= Taki183, Tracey 168, T-Kid170
STIK OR TWIST= 6 and 3
MASON KNOWS= Hublot:Less. Prada:More. Skull Rings:Less. Versace Balaclava:More. Yacht:More.
PURE EVIL: 9+7=16, 7+8=15, 12+5=17, 6+8=14
D*FACE: 16-12=4, 12-6=6, 19-14=5, 14-11=3
BOTJOY: 1=C, 2=E, 3=A, 4=F, 5=D, 6=B.
CRANIO CHALLENGE:
0, **5**, 10, 15, **20**, 25, **30**, 35, 40
11, 22, **33**, 44, **55**, **66**, 77, 88
3, 6, **9**, 12, **15**, 18, **21**, **24**, 27
4, **8**, 12, **16**, 20, 24, **28**, 32
AME TO WIN:

5	+	11	=	16
+		+		+
6	+	3	=	9
=		=		=
11	+	14	=	25

12	+	4	=	16
-		+		-
10	-	2	=	8
=		=		=
2	+	6	=	8

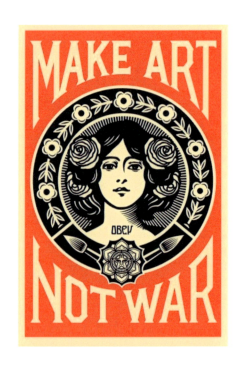

ANSWERS

THINK WITH KASHINK:

```
    S
    e  i  g  h  t
    v        w
    e     e  l  e  v  e  n
    n           l        i
          s     v        n
          f  i  v  e     t  e  n
          x
```

RATS & CATS= Draw 3 rats and 2 cats.
MELTY MADNESS= 10,9,12
COMPLICATED KEITH= 6,4,2
PROBLEMS PAGE
  1. 14
  2. 17
  3. 15
  4. 18
  5. 27
  6. 17
  7. 21

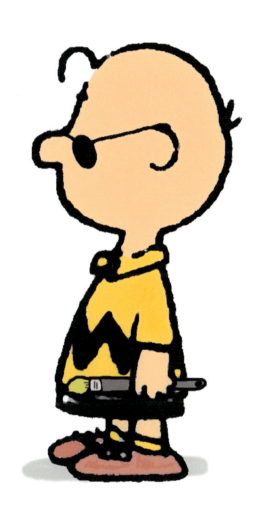

MORE FROM MATT HORRORS

Search on Amazon to find the following rhyming books from Matt Horrors.

- Fiendish Kebabs & Other Ghastly Rhymes
- Electric Eric & Other Tales That Rhyme
- Toxic Chaos & Other Disgusting Tales That Rhyme
- The Battle of East Weezy
- It's a Flat, Flat World

Made in the USA
Columbia, SC
17 January 2025